ABT

4/03

AMERICA AT WAR

KOREAN CONFLICT

Scott Marquette

Rourke Publishing LLC
Vero Beach, Florida 32964

Rourke
Publishing LLC

PHOTO CREDITS:
AP/Wide World Photo: cover, pages 6, 8, 30, 32, 40, 41, 42; Marine Corps Art Collection: pages 4, 18; U.S. Army Center of Military History: pages 10, 14, 20, 23; Defense Visual Information Center: pages 12, 16, 22, 24, 26, 34, 36, 38; Index Stock, page 28.

PRODUCED by Lownik Communication Services, Inc. www.lcs-impact.com
DESIGNED by Cunningham Design

Library of Congress Cataloging-in-Publication Data

Marquette, Scott.
  Korean conflict / Scott Marquette.
     v. cm. – (America at war)
  Includes bibliographical references and index.
  Contents: Introduction: the Cold War turns hot – Map of Korea, 1950 – Timeline – Superpower stand off in Asia – Retreat and counterattack – Reversal and stalemate – Tension and frustration at home – Truce talks begin – Still waiting to reunite.
  ISBN 1-58952-390-3 (hardcover : alk paper)
  1. Korean War, 1950-1953–Juvenile literature. 2. Korean War, 1950-1953–United States–Juvenile literature. 3. United States–Armed Forces–Korea–History–Juvenile literature. 4. World politics–1945–Juvenile literature. [1. Korean War, 1950-1953. 2. World politics–1945-] I. Title. II. America at war (Rourke Publishing)

DS918 .M295 2002
951.904'2–dc21   2002001232

Printed in the USA

Cover Photo:
South Korean soldiers patrol the border between
North and South Korea.

Table of Contents

The U.S. faced communist forces in the rugged land of Korea. Even though the U.S. never declared war, the fighting went on for three years.

Introduction

The Cold War Turns Hot

The end of World War II in 1945 did not bring peace. Instead, America faced a new kind of war. The Soviet Union and China tried to spread **communism** around the world. The U.S. used threats and diplomacy to stop them. At stake was a possible nuclear war. This **Cold War** threatened the entire world.

In 1950, the Cold War turned hot in Asia. In the tiny, rugged land of Korea, U.S. forces squared off against the communists. It was the first time the United Nations sent troops to a conflict. And it was the first war in which both sides had nuclear weapons.

The fight lasted three years. But the U.S. never declared war in Korea. And the war has never been officially ended. When the war was over, not much had changed. The Korean Conflict is sometimes called "The Forgotten War." Almost a half century later, two mighty armies still face each other in Korea.

This memorial in Washington, D.C. commemorates the sacrifices made by U.S. soldiers in Korea.

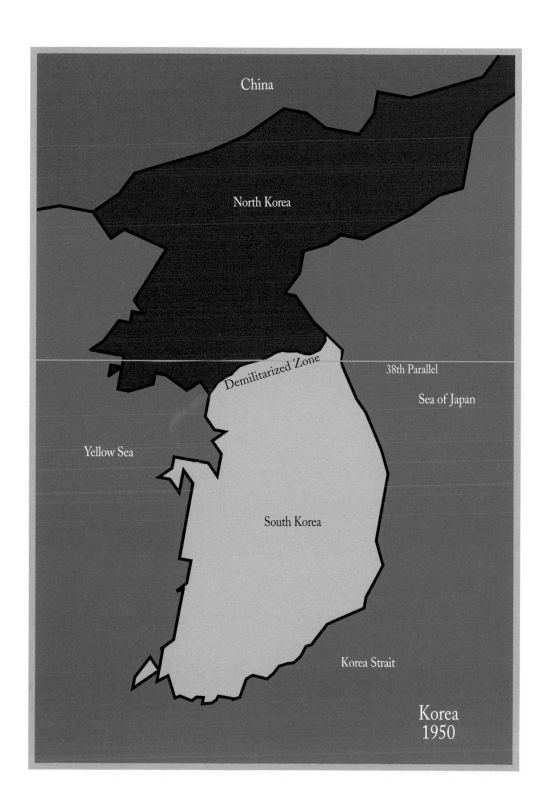

China

North Korea

Demilitarized Zone

38th Parallel

Sea of Japan

Yellow Sea

South Korea

Korea Strait

Korea
1950

KOREAN CONFLICT TIMELINE

1945
September 9: U.S. accepts Japanese surrender south of the 38th Parallel

1948
August 15: Republic of Korea declared in south

September 9: Communist regime declared in north

1950
June 25: North Korea invades South Korea; UN demands North Korea return to its border.

June 30: President Truman sends U.S. troops to Korea

September 15–19: U.S. troops land at Inchon, break through Pusan perimeter

September 27: U.S. crosses 38th Parallel into North Korea

October: UN forces reach Chinese border

November 1: China attacks UN forces

1951
March: Battle lines established along 38th Parallel

April 11: Truman relieves MacArthur of command

July 10: Truce talks begin

1953
July 27: Truce agreement signed

Superpower Stand Off In Asia

After World War II, the U.S. was at conflict with the Soviet Union. The **Soviets** kept control of the nations they had captured in the war. They imposed communism on these nations. At the same time, China became a communist nation. The two huge countries were now allies.

America was alarmed. It saw communism as a threat to freedom. The U.S. was afraid that the Soviets would try to spread communism all over the world. President Harry Truman declared that the U.S. would fight to stop the Soviets from taking any more countries. One of the nations at risk was Korea.

Korea had known war for much of its history. The land sat between two mighty rivals, China and Japan. For hundreds of years, both nations struggled to rule Korea. China had controlled Korea since 1637. In 1910, Japan took over Korea. It drove China out and claimed the nation for itself.

Japan ruled Korea until the end of World War II.

U.S. troops went to Korea to keep communist forces from taking over the country.

In 1945, the **Allies** freed Korea from Japan. Japan surrendered to the Soviets in the north and the U.S. in the south. The U.S. and Soviets agreed to divide the nation between them at 38 degrees north latitude. This line is known as the **38th Parallel**. The Soviets **occupied** the north while the U.S. occupied the south.

Everyone wanted to see Korea go on as one nation. But the Soviets and the U.S. argued about how **reunification** should happen. The Soviets set up a government in the north. They would not let anyone cross the 38th Parallel.

The **United Nations** (UN) called for free elections. But the north refused to participate. The south held an election. In August 1948, a new nation was established in the south. A month later, a communist state was declared in the north. Korea was now formally cut in two.

By 1949, all U.S. and Soviet troops were gone. But the Soviets helped North Korea build and train a large army. In 1950, North Korea tried to reunite the country by force. With the help

Harry S. Truman

Vice president Harry Truman became president in 1945 when Franklin Roosevelt died. At first he did not know if he could do the job. But he helped America through the end of World War II and the early Cold War years. He was known as a tough, honest man.

President Harry S. Truman led the U.S. during two wars: the end of World War II and the Korean Conflict.

of Soviet weapons, northern forces swept into the south on June 25. The South Korean army was too small and weak to resist. Three days later, northern troops took the capital of the south, **Seoul**. The southern army was in full **retreat**. It looked as if South Korea would soon fall to the communists.

U.S. forces fought alongside troops of 16 other nations as part of the United Nations mission to Korea.

Retreat and Counterattack

After World War II, the UN was formed to keep nations from waging wars of **aggression**. The north's **invasion** of South Korea was just that kind of conflict. The UN called on North Korea to stop the invasion. But its pleas were ignored.

The UN voted to use force to rescue South Korea. In all, 16 nations sent troops. But most of the military might belonged to the U.S. America sent ships and planes to support South Korea. But the south needed more help. Soldiers were needed on the ground.

Led by General Douglas MacArthur, the U.S. Army arrived in early July 1950. But the U.S. troops were too few and had too little training. By late July, the northern army had pushed the UN and South Korean troops to the tip of Korea at Pusan. There, the communist advance was finally stopped. But the North was in control of most of the country. It kept up a fierce attack.

When MacArthur had enough troops, he devised a bold plan. He sent troops by sea to land at **Inchon**, near Seoul. This way he could attack his enemy from two sides. On September 15, 1950, the

U.S. troops launch a surprise attack at Inchon. The bold move forced the communists back to the North.

U.S. troops attacked at Inchon. At the same time, the U.S. made a major push at Pusan. The fighting was intense. But the U.S. soon broke the northern line at Pusan. In a few days, Seoul was retaken. The northern army was almost destroyed. It retreated back across the 38th Parallel.

Before the war, the North had a fleet of Soviet fighter planes. But when North Korean jets attacked a U.S. ship in late June, U.S. bombers struck back. Within two weeks, the entire northern air force was destroyed.

Now, North Korea wanted to end the war. It said it would accept the old border at the 38th Parallel. But the U.S. would not give up so easily. Along with South Korea, it decided to reunify Korea under a democratic government. The North warned that China would join the war if UN troops attacked. The U.S. ignored that threat.

Winter War in the Mountains

The winters of 1950 and 1951 were a terrible time for U.S. troops. Bitter cold and snow made it hard to fight. Rugged, mountainous land in the north slowed their movements. They were outnumbered by enemy troops. It was some of the worst fighting in U.S. history.

*U.S. troops suffered terribly during the bitter winters
of 1950 and 1951.*

In October, UN forces pressed north across the 38th Parallel. Little was left of the North Korean army. It was forced back by advancing U.S. troops. In less than two months, UN forces reached the Yalu River at the border between Korea and China. They planned a final attack to finish the North Koreans. But they had a surprise in store.

United Nations forces were stunned by the entry of the Chinese into the war in late 1950.

Reversal and Stalemate

With the North Korean army nearly finished, MacArthur believed victory was at hand. He believed his plan to reunify Korea would be a success. Even if China entered the war, he thought U.S. forces would be strong enough to keep Chinese troops out of Korea.

But China had already sent troops to Korea in secret. In November 1950, just as a fierce winter was setting in, China attacked. The 300,000 Chinese troops far outnumbered the UN force. The UN troops had no choice but to retreat. Some left by sea. But several Marine and Army **divisions** were trapped inland. They had to fight their way back to the south. The Chinese gave them no time to rest.

Douglas MacArthur

General MacArthur was a great hero of World War II. His brilliant leadership broke the might of Japan. Americans hoped he could win in Korea, too. But he was not prepared for China to attack.

General Douglas MacArthur (seated) led U.S. forces in Korea. He was a popular figure back home, but got in trouble with President Truman.

The UN troops froze in the harsh cold. They killed tens of thousands of Chinese troops. But they could not resist China's overwhelming advance.

Then China attacked Seoul. UN forces had to leave the city. The capital of South Korea was once again in communist hands. In the south, the UN forces were better able to fight back. China lost thousands of men. But the communists were still able to force the UN troops back across the 38th Parallel.

By January 1951, UN troops were able to regroup. China was weakened by its heavy battle losses. MacArthur

After retreating, UN forces pushed the Chinese back over the 38th Parallel.

was able to launch another attack. U.S. jets and tanks helped push the communists back. Where the Chinese did not retreat, they were

The massive destruction caused by the war forced many Koreans to flee their homes.

slaughtered. By mid March, UN forces were able to take back Seoul. In days, the communists were forced back to the 38th Parallel once more.

After nearly winning the war, UN forces were barely able to avoid disaster. But China's entry into the war changed everything. To reunify Korea, the U.S. would have to declare war on China. It was a move Truman would not make. Too many American lives would be lost. There was even the risk of nuclear war with the Soviets. The U.S. would have to settle for keeping North Korea from invading the south. The dream of reunifying Korea would have to be abandoned.

MacArthur did not agree. He felt that the U.S. should fight the Chinese army back. He even wanted to attack China itself. He made his views known to the public. This made Truman very angry. He removed MacArthur from command of UN forces in Korea.

It seemed that soldiers had just come back from World War II when Americans had to send men to fight in Korea.

Tension and Frustration at Home

Most Americans stood behind the war effort in Korea. They felt the communists had to be stopped. Many feared that the Soviets would take over the world. They saw communism as a threat to freedom. America saw its role as the chief defender of the **free world**.

And yet, Americans were tired of war. Life was just starting to get back to normal after World War II. That war had cost many lives. There had been shortages of things like food, cars, and other goods. Now, the U.S. economy was booming. People were enjoying the best **standard of living** in history.

People got better jobs and made more money. More people than ever could own their own homes. Inventions like television, modern refrigerators, and superhighways made life easier and more fun. After the long, gloomy war years, people just wanted to enjoy themselves. They did not look forward to life in wartime.

The Korean Conflict was different from past wars. The U.S. did not declare war against North Korea or the Soviets. To declare war, the president has to

In the 1950s, Americans were beginning to enjoy a rich lifestyle. Many did not want to think about war.

get the consent of Congress. But Truman was sending troops to support a UN mission. Instead of a war, the conflict was called a "police action."

As the war in Korea went on, frustration grew. Americans were shocked when China forced U.S. troops to retreat. They had expected a quick, clear victory. Instead, the war seemed to drag on forever. More men had to be **drafted** into the military.

Unlike World War II, it was not clear what it would take to win this war. Some people wanted to use atom bombs in Korea. They thought the U.S. should use its most deadly weapon to force the Soviets to back down. But others felt the use of atom bombs would lead to a nuclear war with the Soviets. Such a war might destroy American cities. To them, saving South Korea was not worth the risk.

The Red Menace

Many Americans were afraid that communists (or Reds) were taking over the nation. Congress held hearings to expose "secret reds." A few real communists were caught. But many innocent people were also accused.

While fighting communists in Korea, many Americans were afraid of communists at home. Congress held hearings to uncover secret communists in the U.S. government.

After 1951, there seemed to be no progress in the war. Truman was not as popular as he had been. Many people were angry that he had fired MacArthur. The great World War II general Dwight Eisenhower ran for president. He promised he would go to Korea to end the conflict. Truman's party lost the White House in 1952.

The helicopter was first used in wartime in Korea.

Truce Talks Begin

By spring 1951, the Korean Conflict had reached a stalemate. Neither the UN nor the communists wanted to take the risks needed to defeat the other side. Both sides were now willing to go back to the pre-war border. In June, the Soviets indicated that **truce** talks might be possible. In response, the U.S. offered to start **negotiations**. Both North Korea and China accepted the offer.

Truce talks began on July 10, 1951. The talks did not go smoothly. The UN only wanted to end the war with honor. But China and North Korea had other ideas. They hoped to gain at the conference table what they could not win in battle. The communists tried to embarrass the UN **delegates**. Communist delegates stalled and caused delays. They hoped the UN would give in to them just to get some progress made. They also used the talks as a showcase for communist **propaganda**.

While the talks took place, the fighting slowed. Neither side launched a major attack on the other. Instead, both used the lull in fighting to rebuild

U.S. soldiers capture Chinese troops. Despite some UN victories, fighting had bogged down by 1953.

their forces. In late August, the communists walked out on the talks. The U.S. launched an attack and gained some ground. The defeat brought China and North Korea back to the talks.

The truce talks went on for another year and a half. The communists wanted to get back land they had lost in battle. They also wanted all their prisoners of war back. But many of the prisoners did not want to return to communist rule.

Meanwhile the fight continued. Both sides dug in along the 38th Parallel. Both sides had heavy losses. But neither side made much progress.

In 1953, both sides had changes of leaders. In January, Dwight Eisenhower was sworn in as U.S. president. He threatened to renew fighting if a truce did not come soon. Then in March the Soviet dictator Josef Stalin died. The changes helped end the war.

Finally, on July 27, 1953, a truce was signed. It called for both sides to pull back from the

Modern War in an Ancient Land

Most Koreans were farmers. They lived much as their ancestors had for centuries. But because of U.S. and Soviet weapons, the Korean Conflict was a very modern war. Both sides used jet fighter planes, missiles, and armored vehicles.

U.S. fighter planes dominated the skies over Korea.

battle line. The space between them would become a **demilitarized zone**. No army could enter without breaking the truce. The truce did not end the war, though. The two sides agreed to hold separate peace talks.

Those talks took years to occur. No peace agreement has ever been reached. The war that was never formally declared has never formally ended. U.S. troops are still in South Korea today. Across the 38th Parallel, they still face a strong North Korean army. For all the thousands of lives lost, the Korean Conflict changed almost nothing.

Korean delegates signed a truce ending the war on July 27, 1953.

Still Waiting to Reunite

For more than fifty years, Korea has been a land split in two. After the war, both nations tried to rebuild what the war had destroyed. Under its ruler, Kim Il Sung, North Korea became a **dictatorship**. Kim held all power in the nation. Most of the nation's wealth went to the military. The government ran the economy. It received much aid from the Soviets. But North Korea did not see much progress.

South Korea took a different path. Though its government was shaky after the war, it has stayed democratic. **Free enterprise** was encouraged. Many modern factories were built. U.S. aid and loans helped South Korea rebuild. Today, the standard of living for most South Koreans is much better than for people in the North. But both nations have suffered because of the conflict. Both have had to keep large armies.

Korea was split because of Cold War tension between the U.S. and the Soviets. In 1990, the Soviet Union fell. The Cold War was over. But the conflict between North and South Korea remained.

*Today, North Koreans regard Kim Il Sung
as a great hero.*

Its old allies were trying new ways. But North Korea was still a communist dictatorship. Kim even tried to get nuclear weapons. Both sides have had to be ready to go to war again at any time. In that way, time in Korea sometimes seems frozen in the 1950s.

U.S. and South Korean troops still patrol the demilitarized zone that divides the country in two.

In 2000, North Korean leader Kim Jong Il (right) and South Korean President Kim Dae-Jung (left) signed a historic declaration to work toward unification of the country.

Recently, there has been new hope that Korea may reunite. Kim Il Sung died in 1994. His son, Kim Jong Il, took power. In 2000, he met with leaders in South Korea. They talked of ending the conflict. But there is still no formal peace between North and South. The goal of reunification still seems very far away.

Americans were not happy with the how the war

ended. There was no clear-cut victory like there was in both World Wars. The loss of 37,000 American lives had achieved little. Most people just wanted to forget the war. But America would soon fight again in Asia. The war in Vietnam would be another undeclared war against communism. It would be an even greater disaster for the U.S.

Fifty years later, we are starting to remember "The Forgotten War." Even though it was not a simple war, Americans fought bravely. Many gave their lives for the cause of freedom. If America had not fought, all of Korea would have fallen to communism. The U.S. showed it would stand up to its enemies even in the face of atom bombs. Today, Americans still sacrifice to keep South Korea free.

Kim Il Sung

Kim Il Sung fought against the Japanese in World War II. In 1945, he helped the Soviets start a communist state in North Korea. He was the dictator of North Korea for nearly fifty years.

Two U.S. Army soldiers stop to discuss their next move during a regular patrol of the demilitarized zone.

Further Reading

Benson, Sonia G. *Korean War: Biographies.* Gale Group, 2001.

Dolan, Edward F. *America in the Korean War.* Millbrook Press, 1998.

Hyung Kyu Shin. *Remembering Korea 1950: A Boy Soldier's Story.* University of Nevada Press, 2001.

McGowen, Tom. *The Korean War (A First Book).* Franklin Watts, 1993.

Sherrow, Victoria. *Joseph McCarthy and the Cold War.* Blackbirch Marketing, 1998.

Stein, R. Conrad. *The Korean War: "The Forgotten War."* Enslow Publishers, 1994.

Warren, James A. *Cold War: The American Crusade Against Communism, 1945-1990.* Lothrop Lee & Shepard, 1996.

Websites to Visit

"Korean War," Microsoft® Encarta® Online Encyclopedia 2001 http://encarta.msn.com

Life In Korea: Korean War Tribute www.lifeinkorea.com/koreanwar.cfm

Glossary

aggression — unprovoked attack, as of one nation against another

Allies — the World War II alliance of Britain, the United States, and the Soviet Union

Cold War — conflict between the United States and the Soviet Union between 1945 and 1990

Communism — political system based on the idea that the government should make all economic decisions on behalf of the people

delegates — official representatives sent to a meeting

demilitarized zone — area along the 38th Parallel into which military forces cannot enter

dictatorship — government in which all power is in the hands of a single ruler

divisions — military units big enough to act on their own in battle

drafted — compelled to serve in the military

free enterprise — operation of business without government control

free world — nations not controlled by communists during the Cold War

Inchon — port city on the west coast of South Korea

invasion — military takeover of a place or nation

negotiations — talks where parties to a conflict try to agree on a settlement

occupied — controlled by a foreign military force

propaganda — spreading ideas that support a cause

Reds — nickname for members of the communist party

retreat — movement of an army back from the lines of battle

reunification — bringing a divided country together again as one nation

Seoul — the capital of South Korea

Soviets — Russian for "council;" used to refer to people and things from the Soviet Union.

standard of living — the ability of a person or group to provide for its own needs and comfort

38th Parallel — 38 degrees north latitude; the map line used to divide Korea into north and south

truce — cease-fire between armies

United Nations — an organization of nations formed after World War II to prevent war and promote international cooperation; also known as the UN

Index